Welcome
TO THE

GRIEF
CLUB

BECAUSE YOU DON'T HAVE TO
GO THROUGH IT ALONE

JANINE KWOH

WORKMAN PUBLISHING · NEW YORK

Library of Congress Cataloging-in-Publication Data
Names: Kwoh, Janine, author.
Title: Welcome to the grief club : because you don't have to go through it
   alone / Janine Kwoh.
Identifiers: LCCN 2021017318 | ISBN 9781523511716 (hardcover) | ISBN
   9781523515332 (ebook)
Subjects: LCSH: Grief. | Loss (Psychology)
Classification: LCC BF575.G7 K96 2022 | DDC 155.9/37--dc23
LC record available at https://lccn.loc.gov/2021017318

ISBN 978-1-5235-1171-6

Cover design by Janine Kwoh

Workman books are available at special discounts when purchased in bulk for premiums and sales promotions as well as for fundraising or educational use. Special editions or book excerpts can also be created to specification. For details, contact the Special Sales Director at specialmarkets@workman.com.

Workman Publishing Co., Inc., 225 Varick Street, New York, NY 10014-4381

workman.com

WORKMAN is a registered trademark of Workman Publishing Co., Inc.

Printed in China
First printing December 2021

10 9 8 7 6 5 4 3 2 1

for Nap,
who made my tiny patch of world
so much brighter

Welcome to the Grief Club. This club is for those who have loved deeply and lost greatly. And even though there are no magic fixes or ways to speed up or rewind to the part where it's all OK again, we hope there is comfort in community and in knowing that you don't have to go through it alone.

Though our losses and experiences are all unique, there are those of us who get it— we really do. We know what it's like for everything to fundamentally and irreparably change in an instant. We know that grief doesn't come in anything resembling stages, and that you can be OK one moment and sobbing in the grocery store the next. We know that sometimes there's no harder question to answer than "How are you?"

We don't have answers, but we'll listen without judgment or platitudes. We don't have road maps, but it's often less scary to be lost together. And if you can't see the light at the end of the tunnel yet, we'll show up waving flashlights until you do, for as long as it takes.

From one card-carrying member to another, I know that this is really hard.

You will get through this, I promise.

A heartfelt thank you to all of the Grief Club members who shared photos, stories, and memories with me for this book. You are the inspiration for many of the people and examples illustrated in these pages.

Contents

INTRODUCTION

I lost my partner, Nap, when we were both in our late twenties. He was brilliant, curious, and fun-loving—always the first to hug someone hello and the last to leave the dance floor. In our quieter moments together, he was thoughtful and earnest, and never made me feel like I should be anyone different than who I was. He was flawed and complicated, and one of the most unique souls I've ever known. He was my friend, my refuge, and a consistent bit of goodness in my life.

Nap died unexpectedly in 2016. He was the first person I loved who died, and I was the only person my age I knew to have lost a partner. The experience of losing him and grieving his death has been harder, longer, more complicated, and lonelier than I could have imagined.

I don't think I'll ever have the words to fully convey what the initial period after he died was like; the best description I can come up with is that it didn't really feel like living. It wasn't just that I had never felt such pain or sadness, but that it didn't seem physically possible to sustain the depth and breadth of emotions that pummeled me relentlessly and in dizzying combinations—longing, guilt, rage, despair, numbness, and fatigue—even as the outside world continued to hum along as usual. It was surreal. It still is. I mercifully don't remember large swaths of that first year without him, but I do remember that I kept thinking I just wanted to catch a glimpse of him—at the neighborhood coffee shop or on the other side of the street, anywhere—so I could know that he was still in the world, because it was inconceivable that he wasn't.

I often talk about grief as one of the most isolating experiences, despite it being one of the most common. As I write this, it feels like I'm straddling two parallel universes—the one in which I am a happy and well-adjusted friend, sister, romantic partner, and business owner;

and the one in which I am all of those things but also still bruised and broken in countless invisible places. This second world spills over with memories, ghosts, fears, love, and so much grief that it sometimes still feels impossible and uncontainable, even years later. I cry and laugh and forget and remember, over and over again.

I imagine all of us walking around in our own personal parallel universes with our unseen broken places, wondering if we're the only ones. I think it's worth opening up our worlds and wounds to one another—I suspect that they are more similar than we think.

This book is for anyone who has lost someone they care about. Consider this a welcome to the club that no one ever wants to join but so many of us end up needing.

This book is undeniably steeped in my own grief, but it's not about me or a retelling of my personal loss. It's about all of the surprising, confusing, brutal, funny, and downright bizarre parts of grief that a lot of us experience but don't often discuss.

This book is about unadulterated grief. It's about bearing witness to the enormity of what has transpired. It acknowledges that there's no way to bypass the hard and painful parts, but also reminds us that we are not alone, even in our darkest moments.

This book is about how grief is a natural response to losing a love, and how we need to give ourselves permission to grieve for as long as— and in whichever ways—we need to. It is an assurance that the things we feel that surprise us or seem strange are often common and always valid.

This book is about how grief isn't a hurdle that we eventually overcome, but rather something that we will always carry as part of us. It's about how grief doesn't go away, but tends to soften over time. It's about the messy, slow work of rebuilding a life when the one we had is no longer an option.

This is a book about how humor and joy inevitably fight their way to the surface in the bleakest of times, and how they help us to survive.

This is a book about love.

I wrote this book because it's what I wish someone had given me in the depths of my grief. I wrote it because people who had loved and lost before me did tell me some of these things, and their words were a lifeline. I wrote it because the world went maddeningly on after Nap died, and I want everyone who reads this to know he existed, and that he mattered.

I wrote this book because I believe there is power in standing in your story—the whole story—and comfort in seeing parts of your story reflected in those of others. Writing it made me feel less lonely. I hope reading it does the same for you, and that it brings some nods of recognition, a smile and even a few laughs, and a spot of comfort in hard times.

Love,
Janine ♡

this book

me in my
grief bubble

you in your
grief bubble

A Guide to Reading This Book

I wish there was an instruction manual for grief. I wish I could share step-by-step directions that tell you exactly what to do next, and that you could flip to the last page to see what it's supposed to look like at the end. But this would be impossible, since each experience of grief is unique.

So, this book is not a how-to guide on grief. Rather, it is a collage of experiences and perspectives I've gathered over the years, both hard-won through my own loss and from other Grief Club members who have generously shared with me. It also draws from and builds upon the grief work of other writers, artists, and professionals (for credits/sources, please visit workman.com/griefclub). I fully expect that this book will fall short of capturing the entirety of anyone's experience, but I hope that everyone can recognize some of themselves in its pages.

There are many experiences that do not involve death but can trigger similar emotions, for example: going through a breakup or divorce, moving to a new home or city, changing or losing a job, or sustaining an injury or illness. It's possible that parts of this book will speak to those navigating a range of different experiences that involve loss, but the term "Grief Club" as it's used in this book refers specifically to those who are grieving a death. This is not to minimize or invalidate other types of loss, but to create a dedicated space for those grieving the death of a loved one, as they are the primary audience for whom I wrote this book.

If you love someone who is grieving, I hope this book helps you understand what they may be going through, and in turn gives you ideas for how to better support them.

Grief does not progress linearly, so this book doesn't either. Each section offers a smattering of thoughts, affirmations, and examples in response to questions that many of us have throughout the grieving process, especially those that often go unasked or unacknowledged.

You can read this book cover to cover, jump to the section that interests you most, open it up to a random page, skip over some parts, or bookmark others to revisit later. Some topics will be more or less relevant, depending on your individual circumstances and where you are in your grief. I hope you find this book to be a gentle companion and a comforting resource. I hope it is a voice that says, *I see you and you are not alone*. Please take what's useful, and leave what's not.

OTHER SUPPORTS

Each loss comes with its own specific circumstances and special considerations. Who you lost and how they died will shape your grieving process. This book doesn't explore in depth the different types of loss and their implications, including but not limited to: a loved one who is missing, a loved one living with a brain injury or dementia, grieving multiple losses, violent deaths, anticipated deaths, sudden deaths, pregnancy losses, suicides, and accidental overdoses. I also don't explicitly discuss pet loss. This is not because these types of losses aren't important to explore, but on the contrary, because I felt that I couldn't do them justice, given the length and format of this book, and in some cases, my lack of personal experience.

If you're looking for more information on specific types of loss, I encourage you to seek resources that are out there. If you feel like you could use some help navigating your grief, please visit workman.com/griefclub for possible sources of support.

Please seek professional help if you're struggling to cope with your grief, or if you are struggling with substance use, depression, and/or other behavioral health issues, or if you have thoughts of hurting yourself or others: US Substance Abuse and Mental Health Services Administration (SAMHSA) National Helpline: 1-800-662-4357; US National Suicide Prevention Hotline: 1-800-273-8255; Crisis Text Line: crisistextline.org.

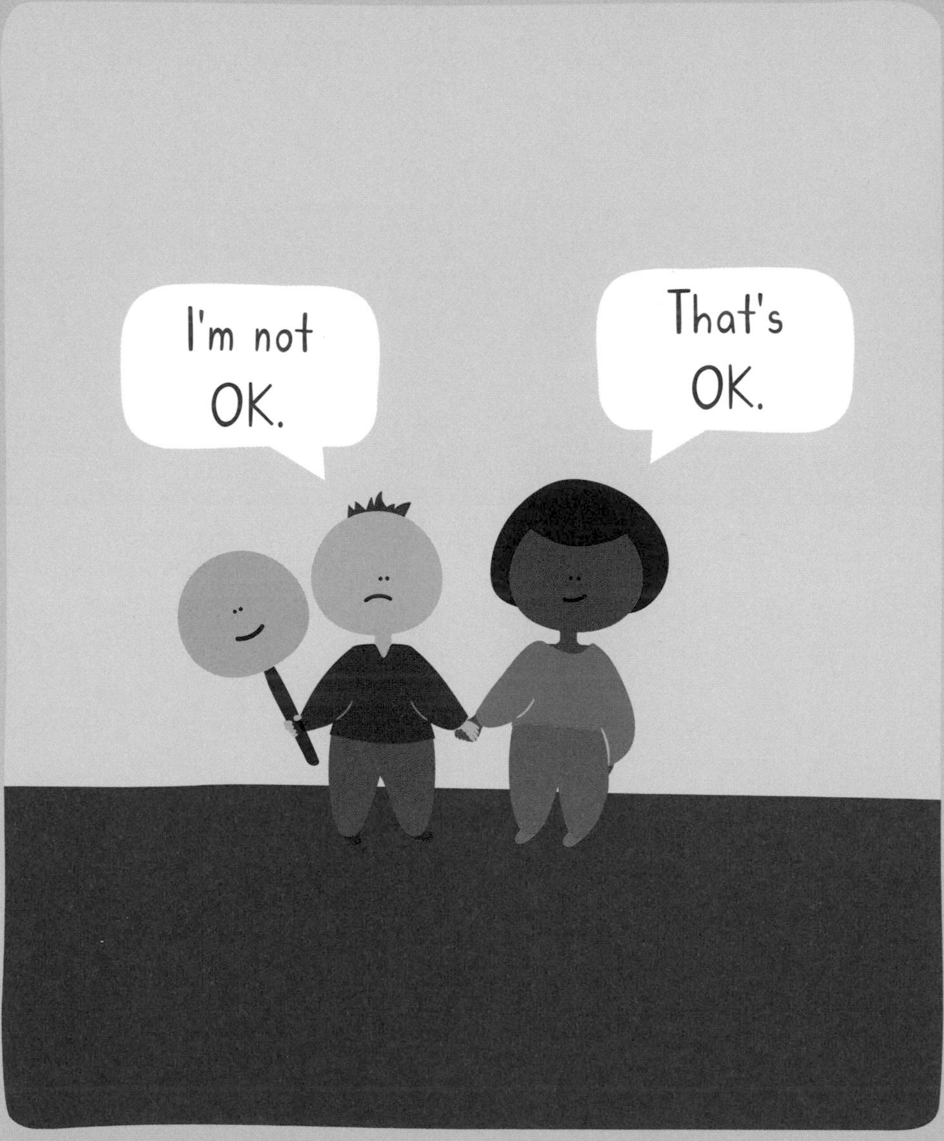
I'm not OK.
That's OK.

WELCOME TO THE GRIEF CLUB

Someone you care about has died.

You are now a member of the Grief Club—the club that no one wants to be part of but is here for you when you need it. Some of us are grieving family members; others are grieving partners and friends. Some of our loved ones were young and others were older. Some of their deaths were anticipated, while others were unexpected. What we have in common as Grief Club members is that we have all loved and lost.

It can seem as if no one understands what you're going through. You may be wondering if what you're experiencing is "normal," or how you can possibly survive this loss. As fellow unwilling Grief Club members, we get it. We really, really do. While grief is different for everyone, we know that whatever you're feeling is valid, and that while losing someone you care about is excruciatingly hard, you will get through this.

Welcome to the Grief Club—we're so sorry that you're here.

GRIEF CLUB
CLUBHOUSE RULES

MEMBERSHIP

- Club membership is open to anyone who has experienced a significant loss.*

- Club capacity is unlimited at any given time.

- Membership enrollment is automatic.

- Members of all ages, races and ethnicities, genders, sexual orientations, abilities, nationalities, religions, and backgrounds are welcome here.

MEMBER CONDUCT

- Members are expected to grieve on their own timelines and in any manner of their choosing.

- The experiencing of all feelings is permitted and encouraged.

- Crying is allowed at all hours. Not crying is also allowed.

- Frequent use of profanity is acceptable.

- Proper attire is required. This includes but is not limited to: head-to-toe sweats and whatever clothing is closest.

- Please keep in mind that this is the Grief Club, NOT the Grief Olympics—any comparison of grief is strictly prohibited.

- Any person who utters the phrase "Everything happens for a reason" will be removed immediately from the premises.

- Existing club members are encouraged to extend a welcome and their condolences to new members.

Thank you for keeping this an inclusive, supportive, albeit slightly sad, and judgment-free environment.

—Management

*What constitutes a "significant loss" is defined by each individual member. No external verification of membership eligibility is necessary.

FUCK YOU, UNIVERSE

and anyone who tells you that this is all part of a bigger plan. Because if it is, it's a shitty fucking plan and I'd like to punch whoever's plan this is.

This is the absolute pits.

They died, but somehow the rest of the world continues on—people are still stressing over deadlines, complaining about their commute, and making brunch plans, as if no one noticed this new gaping void in the universe. Your life as you know it has been shattered, and they're wondering if you can send over your meeting notes by the end of the day.

You may feel as if you're living in a parallel, broken universe that no one seems to acknowledge, and that you're reeling from a loss that no one else sees. This can make you want to grab someone—anyone—and shake them until they recognize your new reality. It can make you want to pull them into your universe so they have no choice but to experience for themselves the pain you're in.

Our losses don't impact others as deeply, even if we sometimes wish they would. On top of that, the way we approach grief as a society doesn't help: We're not accustomed to, and therefore not adept at, talking about and dealing with grief. Some people won't acknowledge your loss because it makes them uncomfortable, or they're afraid of saying the wrong things, or they don't want to make you sad by bringing it up. Others will offer their condolences and support immediately after the death, but oftentimes will stop acknowledging it after the first few weeks or months.

An unintended consequence of the whiplash speed at which everyone else returns to life as usual is that it can seem as if the loss you are grieving isn't important. You may feel like you should be grieving less, or at least more privately, and moving through your grief more quickly than you are.

Regardless of other people's reactions, the only thing that matters is that this death is significant to *you*. They were an important part of your life, and now they're gone—it is natural for you to feel a deep sense of loss.

Sometimes, a confirmation of the supreme shittiness of the situation can be oddly more comforting than any platitudes or words of wisdom. So here is your affirmation, in case you need to hear it:

Supremely Unhelpful Things That People Say to Grieving People

What people say:

Everything happens for a reason.

It was their time.

Well, everyone dies eventually.

You should try dating again.

At least they died quickly.

At least you got to spend five years with them.

At least they were old.

At least you got to say goodbye.

On the bright side, you're still young and can remarry.

On the bright side, you can always have another child.

They're in a better place now.

What the grieving person might hear:

You are more upset than you should be.

You should be relieved— it could have been worse.

What Grief Can Feel Like:
Some Possible Metaphors

Floating outside of your body and watching it go through the day

Sinking in quicksand

Being on fire without anyone noticing

Wandering around in a fog

Did I eat today?
What month is it?
What do I do now?

Having a
physical hole
in your heart

Getting thrown around by
waves that come and go
without warning (not gentle,
lapping waves but giant, crashing ones)

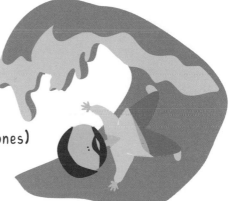

THE TEARFUL
TORNADO

Riding a roller coaster that is out of control

Grief is lonely,
but you are not alone.

We can't fully experience and share in one another's losses. No one else is living your grief or has had your loss, even if you are grieving the same person. Your relationship was unique, and so your loss is unique. What you miss about them, what you wish you had or hadn't said, the memories you made or could have made together—these belong only to you.

The solitude of grief can quickly turn into loneliness. It can be almost impossible to explain the magnitude and experience of your loss to others. Even when you do talk about your grief, some people will become uncomfortable. Others might avoid you altogether—you may notice your coworkers giving you a wide berth at the office or your friends leaving you out of plans. While they may be wanting to give you space, this can make you feel even more lonely.

No Grief Club member can know your loss as intimately as you do, but we do know what it's like to lose someone we love. So when it feels like you've hit rock bottom (or a hundred miles below that), know that you're not sitting in the muck alone.

CARE INSTRUCTIONS

Be gentle with yourself.

For best results, feel things deeply.

THERE IS NO RIGHT OR WRONG WAY TO GRIEVE

There is no universal yardstick by which to measure and judge your grieving process. That said, it's common to feel as if you are not grieving "correctly"— you are too sad or not sad enough; you should have moved on by now or you are moving on too quickly.

What a relief it would be to know that you are grieving on schedule, in correct and healthy ways, and with maximum expediency. But for better or worse, there is no way to ace grief. On the flip side, there is no way to fail at it. Anything goes, really.

So give yourself permission to grieve in whichever ways you need, for however long you need to.

AM I GRIEVING CORRECTLY?

Hmm . . . let's see. Did you cry today?

NOPE. Not even one measly little tear.

That's OK. How much or how little you cry isn't the only indication of what you're feeling or how much you care.

Really? It doesn't mean that there's something wrong with me?

That's good—feeling better is a healthy part of moving forward.

I'm actually feeling OK.

I'm so sorry. That's really hard. But also, it's OK to be sad when you miss someone.

Really? But what if I'm, like, REALLY OK? What if I . . .

make new friends

find new family

But what if it's been a long time?

fall in love

have a child

YES—our capacity to love isn't finite. We can hold room for both old and new loves.

Are you sure?

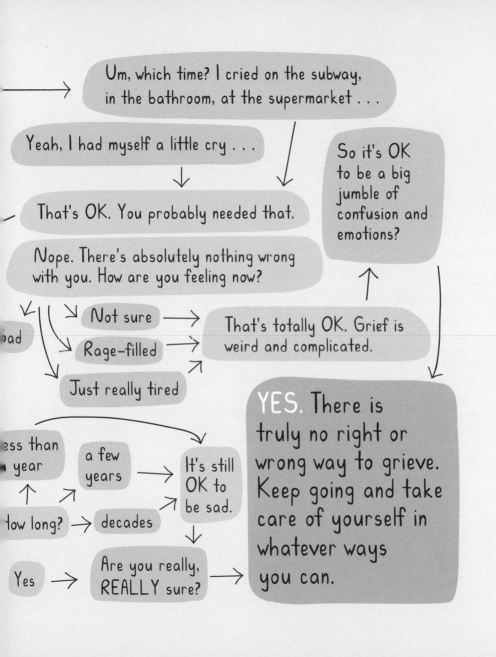

Things Grieving People Do That May Seem Strange but Are Actually Very Common

Find most movies and TV shows unbearable, and then proceed to watch the few "safe" options on repeat

Seek out intimacy and/or sex, or avoid it altogether

Wear the same clothes for weeks on end

Lash out at friends and strangers, like slow walkers or people who breathe too loudly

$?@&*!

Have a hard time mustering up energy to respond to texts, calls, emails, and basically all forms of communication

Talk about it to everyone all the time

Not talk about it at all

Hey, how are you?

Fine, thanks.

Anything new?

Nope.

Have nightmares and/or dreams in which they're still alive

There you are!

Skip out on holidays, celebrations, and basically all social occasions

Save the Date
RSVP: YES
NO ✓

Lose track of time

SMTWTHFS
? ? ?

Why am I crying so much?

They seem really OK.

They must be so much more resilient than me.

Why am I crying so little?

They seem really not OK.

They must be so much more caring than me.

WHAT IS WRONG WITH ME???
I should be grieving more like they are.

We all express our grief differently.

Some of us are incessant criers; others are chronically dry-eyed. Some of us instinctively reach out and seek others for comfort and guidance; others prefer to reflect alone. Some of us find that going back to work consists primarily of hiding out in bathroom stalls; others find that being productive is helpful and they can go back to work without too much disruption. Some of us try dating again or having another child soon after; others don't for a while; some of us never do. All of these reactions can be part of the experience of grief.

Someone's outward expression of grief is not always indicative of how they feel inside. Using others to gauge our own grief can make us feel like we're grieving incorrectly or inappropriately, when really we're all just grieving differently.

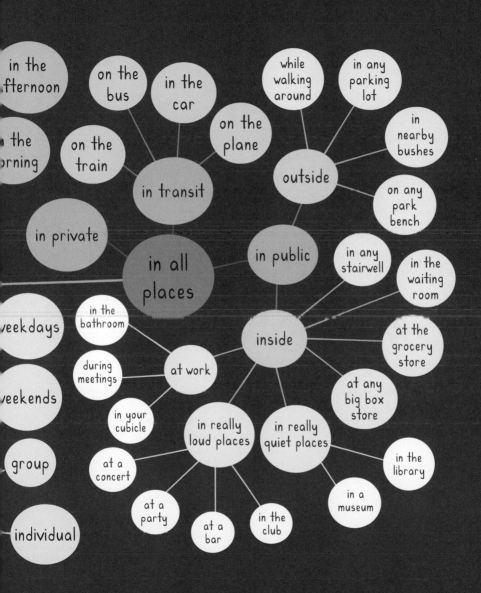

SEARCH

how long is grief supposed to last 🔍

how to write an obituary
funeral flowers coupon code
do I have to write thank-you cards for sympathy cards
can grief cause permanent memory loss
best places to cry at work
things to do on a deathiversary
how to spell deathiversary
how to bring up a dead partner on a first date
how to stop grieving
still grieving one year later is this normal
still grieving ten years later is this normal

Things They Tell You Not to Do in the First Year of Grieving That Many of Us Do*

*It usually turns out OK in the end. There is something comforting about making tangible changes that show you're moving forward in some way, even if that way means your hair is now pink. In a time of so much helplessness, it can be empowering to change your life in a way that is up to you.

Deathiversaries are a thing.

It's common to mark the anniversary of the day someone died—their deathiversary—as an annual day of reflection or remembrance of their life.

How you feel on this anniversary will likely change over time, and sometimes you won't be able to predict how you'll feel on the day until it comes. Some years, it can transport you back to the earliest or most acute periods of your grief, and other years you may only remember after the day has passed. Your mood and body can change in the weeks leading up to and after the deathiversary.

I haven't been sleeping well, I've been getting headaches, and my body has all of these mystery pains—I can't figure out why.

Oh yeah, it's about that time of year again . . .

Deathiversaries can feel like they demand a public, collective display of grief, but you should feel free to spend the day however you like. You can spend it alone, with a few loved ones, or at a larger memorial service. Depending on what is doable for and of interest to you, you can take a couple moments, a few hours, or the whole day to commemorate them or to take care of yourself. It's also OK to not do anything special and to go about your day as you usually would. Do whatever feels most meaningful and healing to you.

Some ideas for what to do on a deathiversary*

Find an excuse to get out of the house

Stay in and watch TV all day

Distract yourself with work

Write something, then share it or keep it private

Plan or attend a memorial ceremony

Opt out of any formal memorial or group event (yes, it is OK for you to do this)

Start a tradition to honor them

Have a get-together with friends and family who also cared deeply about them

Go somewhere without any painful memories

Do something they liked to do, or that you used to do together

*These are also good options for anniversaries, holidays, life milestones, and ordinary days.

More Supremely Unhelpful Things That People Say to Grieving People

What people say:

Wow, did you lose weight? You look great. I'm so jealous.

Are you still sad about that?

How did they die?

They brought it on themselves.

Do you think you could have prevented it if you had done something about it earlier?

I just went through a breakup—I basically feel like a widow too.

What the grieving person might think:

$?@&*!

PERMISSION TO GRIEVE

YOU, **lovely human**, are hereby granted full and absolute permission to engage in any or all of the following activities and/or feelings, concurrently or in no apparent order and without advance warning, for an unrestricted amount of time:

- Talk about it endlessly, or not at all
- Ugly cry in public, at work, with friends, in front of strangers
- Not be your "best self," because it's all too much
- Feel better (without feeling guilty about feeling better)
- Still feel shitty (without feeling guilty about feeling shitty)
- Laugh, preferably really hard
- Be angry—at the universe, bad drivers, self-checkout machines...
- Not know what you want or feel
- Do whatever the fuck you want*
- Just be

SIGNED: **everyone who loves you to tiny bits, even when you're sad and slightly unshowered**

*Except face tattoos—please don't get one. Unless you really, really want to. In which case, we'll go with you and hold your hand and tell you it looks great.

IT'S OK TO FEEL MANY THINGS AT THE SAME TIME

Grief is a jumble of complex, ever-changing, and sometimes clashing emotions—sadness, rage, guilt, anxiety, and numbness, to name a few. Like uninvited, unwanted houseguests, they leave behind messes for you to clean up, keep you awake at all hours, and have no consideration for any plans you may have made for your day. They tend to come and go as they please, usually without any notice or explanation.

In an effort to maintain some semblance of order, we often demand that these rogue feelings follow the house rules (*Sadness is only allowed between the hours of 6 p.m. and 8 p.m.*), or we try to lock them out altogether. But trying to dictate when and how they show up is rarely effective—as much as we would like to, sometimes we just can't control our emotions.

What we *can* do is greet our emotions when they show up (*oh, hello again, Generalized Irritability and Intense Self-Pity*), make a cup of tea, and settle in for a good chat to understand why they're showing up now, and how we might learn to live better together while they're here.

All emotions, welcome or not, can be part of processing this significant life event. And whenever the jumble grows large and unmanageable, give yourself grace for carrying it as best you can.

The self-checkout machine . . .

Why be sad about someone dying when you can be obscenely angry at the self-checkout machine that is inexplicably requiring you to wait for human assistance, just because you tried to buy a stick of deodorant? Your person died, and you smell because you can't be bothered to shower, and now you have to wait for someone to tell this stupid machine that it's OK for you to buy this stupid stick of deodorant so you can stop reeking of grief. The universe hates you, and you hate this checkout machine. Yelling helps a bit, as does the store manager who comes running with their override card in hand.

It is understandable that you are angry; anger is a temporary relief from sadness. There is nowhere to channel sadness—it pools around and engulfs you. Anger, on the other hand, can be directed towards someone or something else. While sadness can leave you feeling helpless, anger gives you something to do—an issue to resolve or a wrong to make right. And even if no one comes running with a solution in hand, it can still feel good to shout, as hard and loudly as you want.*

*While everyone and everything can make you angry, do try to only yell at inanimate objects rather than unsuspecting people with feelings!

and other things that may fill you with rage.

Anyone who has a problem that doesn't involve someone dying

My favorite bakery closed down—
I'm so devastated.

Happy strangers

HA HA! HA HA!

When people act like nothing happened

Hope you have a wonderful weekend!

Anyone who hasn't experienced loss

magical protective bubble against death

The universe

Minor inconveniences

TRAIN DELAYED 3 MINS

The person who died

Why didn't you take better care of yourself?

IS THEIR DEATH MY FAULT?

↓

No, this is not your fault.

↓

But what if . . .

I should have seen it coming?

I could have saved them if only I had acted differently?

I survived when they didn't?

NO. It is still not your fault. We are responsible for taking care of one another the best we can, but it's just not humanly possible to predict the future, or to plan for and prevent every possible bad outcome. Their death is not your fault.

Repeat after me: "This is not my fault."

We think we should have seen it coming. We feel like we could have prevented it if we had only woken them up, or let them sleep in, or been there, or taken another route, or checked in one more time. We replay over and over again all the choices we made and how things could have turned out differently if only we had made better decisions. The what-ifs and if-onlys are agonizing.

But life is unpredictable, sometimes in devastating ways. The fact is that we never know if the decisions we're making are the right ones, even if hindsight makes us feel otherwise. All we can do is act based on the information we have.

Sometimes, terrible random things happen that are impossible to predict or prevent—a plane crash, a flash flood, a branch falling, a brain aneurysm. In cases like these, there's absolutely no way that we could have anticipated what was going to happen.

Other times, it feels like we really could have prevented their death, if only we had been a little more observant, insistent, or attentive—we knew, or should have known, that they were feeling sick, or struggling with alcohol or drugs, or feeling depressed. We berate ourselves for letting that call go to voice mail, or not intervening sooner, or not rushing them to the hospital. But the reality is that we can't always assume the worst and act accordingly. We have to make imperfect judgment calls, and sometimes we get it wrong. This just means that we're human and fallible, not that we're responsible for their death.

There are countless unforeseeable factors that lead to someone's death, many of which are always out of our control. We will never know what would have happened if we did things differently. Even if we did do all the things we wish we had, the outcome might have been the same.

Their death is not your fault. You did not cause this.

What it's like to be on high alert all the time.

Someone important to you has just disappeared forever from the face of the earth. Of course every fiber of your being is screaming "danger"—you know intimately that life-shattering horrors can be around any corner and there's absolutely no way of predicting when they'll show up, or how. The fact that something probably won't happen is no longer reassuring, because you have lived through what it's like when it does. You must maintain constant vigilance, your brain tells you—you must always be on the lookout for any potential sign of danger so you can avoid, or at least be prepared for, the next disaster. So you never have to feel this way again.

Being on high alert all the time after experiencing a trauma is common. But if sustained over time, it takes a toll—it's exhausting and stressful to always be anticipating the worst outcome.

As terrifying as the truth is, life is uncontrollable. You can't keep everyone you love safe, even if you run yourself into the ground trying to do so. It would be impractical to call an ambulance every time someone got a headache, or keep constant tabs on someone who was feeling depressed, or never let anyone get into a car or go swimming or hike a mountain or walk down the stairs. And even if you did, bad things would still happen.

Focus on the parts you can control—do your best to be there for those you care about, and be intentional about how you spend the time you have together.

Checking if they're still alive when they're asleep

Good, they're still breathing.

Checking their recent internet activity for signs of life

phew

Z is currently online

Ending every conversation on a positive note in case one of you dies

My plane is taking off. See you soon!

OK, have a safe flight! I'm sorry for that thing I said last week. Don't die!! Love you!!!

Sending frantic texts when they don't respond immediately the first time

hey u alive???

yup.

ok cool, just checking

Immediately envisioning disaster scenarios whenever someone:

- gets into any moving vehicle
- gets even a little bit sick
- is running late
- doesn't answer their phone
- calls without warning
- enters any circumstance vaguely resembling the one in which another person died

I have a headache.

How bad is it? When did it start? Do you have any other symptoms? Maybe we should go straight to the ER.

Anything (and sometimes everything) can be your grief trigger.

So many objects, places, and experiences can trigger memories or emotions associated with your loss and cause instant waves of grief. Some of these are expected (sorting through their belongings), while others are more surprising (the smell of the shampoo they used). It feels like a pair of grief goggles are strapped to your face, and you can't help but experience everything through the lens of fresh heartbreak.

Triggers can be relentless, especially in the beginning. As time goes on, they often become sporadic and more bittersweet than brutal. But like so many things associated with grief, triggers are unpredictable—you can be unemotional on the first anniversary of their death and then be undone three days later by a sunny patch of sidewalk.

GRIEF TRIG

That stranger's laugh sounds like theirs. tee-hee

They would have loved this movie.

 How can birds be chirping at a time like this?

 It's Thursday.

I used to love crime shows, but now I can't bear to watch any.  LAW & ORDER [DUN DUN]

I wonder what they would have been like at this age. 30

 It's weird to no longer get any more mail for them.

CORN FLAKES I always picked up th brand of cereal for th

They would have hated this party. So, where are you from?

It feels like every woman in this grocery store except me is pregnant.

They would have been six months old today.

Today would have been our tenth anniversary.

They used to wear his perfume all the time.

 I used to always call them to ask for this recipe.

 I always thought they'd walk me down the aisle.

We used to walk around this store together.

I'm the same age today that they were when they died.

This was their favorite song.

 ♪ ooh can't cut loose ♫

 The leaves are changing colors. I can't believe it's already been a whole season since they died.

 That person's nose kind of looks like theirs.

What if I don't feel anything?

Sometimes it can feel as if someone reached into your heart and turned off all your emotions at once. Where you would have felt something before—excitement about future activities, joy in relationships and hobbies, pride in your accomplishments, or worry about disappointing others—you now just feel indifferent. You may feel like an impersonator in your own life, detachedly and cursorily going through the motions of being "you."

The things you delight in, desire, and fear are part of what makes you, you, and feeling disconnected from these things can be disconcerting. It can feel like you have to navigate being someone you don't recognize, on top of adjusting to everything else.

But as bewildering as it can be, feeling numb is common in grief. Your body senses that the full weight of all the emotions triggered by their death would be too debilitating to feel at once. So, like a circuit breaker, it shuts them down before the system overloads. This can give you some additional time to process, especially if you are still absorbing the shock of their death.

At some point, you will begin to feel again. Like a rest stop on a long trek, this numbness isn't a way to bypass feeling our emotions, but a respite that helps us make it through them.

GRIEF MENU

"SERVING THINGS TO DO WHEN YOU DON'T KNOW WHAT TO DO SINCE THEY DIED"

OPEN 24/7

SMALL BITES

MAKE SOME TEA

PAMPER YOURSELF

MAKE YOUR BED

WRITE ABOUT ABSOLUTELY ANYTHING

Today I ate some cheese.

TAKE A SHOWER

TAKEOUT

GO FOR A WALK OR A RUN

RUN AN ERRAND

FIND A BIT OF NATURE

SIT AT A CAFÉ

STAY IN

READ A BOOK THAT TRANSPORTS YOU

☑ MAKE
☐ A
☐ LIST

MEDITATE (OR DON'T, AND JUST WATCH TV)

CUDDLE AN ANIMAL

CLEAN OR ORGANIZE SOMETHING

EAT SOMETHING DELICIOUS

COOK SOMETHING

CREATE SOMETHING (DON'T FEEL LIKE YOU NEED TO FINISH)

SIDES

LISTEN TO A PODCAST

PUT ON A SONG

CALL OR TEXT A FRIEND

Hi!

DAILY SPECIAL: LET GO OF THE IDEA THAT YOU NEED TO BE PRODUCTIVE.

What if I feel OK?

You may feel sad and miss the person you lost, but also feel equipped to contend with your loss. You may wish that they hadn't died, but be able to accept the reality of their death. You may be able to process your grief while also resuming many parts of your life without too much difficulty. Memories of them may make you feel sad, but not overwhelmingly so, or they can be welcome reminders of the time you had together.

If you're not debilitatingly sad, or spending every moment missing and thinking of them, you might wonder: *Is there something wrong with me? Should I be more upset than I am? Does this mean that I didn't care about them that much?*

Feeling OK, even soon after their death, does not mean that you loved them less or that your loss is less consequential. Aside from how much you cared about them, there are so many different factors that shape the nature and intensity of your grief. For example, the circumstances of their death, your personality, your support network, and your life experiences can all contribute to why you're feeling sad but generally fine. Grief is complicated, and it can be impossible to disentangle exactly why you feel the way you do.

At the end of the day, the intensity of your grief is not always commensurate with the size of your loss. It can be true that you love and miss them profoundly, and also that you feel OK.

No one is perfect, even after they die.

They weren't perfect, and they didn't automatically become perfect when they died. None of us are, or do. But after someone dies, it is often taboo to acknowledge their mistakes, personal shortcomings, and/or struggles with mental illness and substance use. It can feel like everyone else is grieving—and expects you to be grieving—a sanitized or simplified version of who they really were.

You may experience a dissonance between others' glowing public tributes (and perhaps even your own) and your knowledge of the less palatable parts of their personality and life that didn't make it into any eulogy or obituary. At the same time, it can feel petty and disrespectful to their memory to still be dwelling on their troubles or the ways they wronged you or let you down.

Someone's imperfections and challenges don't make their life any less worthy of commemorating; they make them human. Maybe they were quick to anger but also eager to lend a helping hand. Maybe they were grappling with mental illness or addiction. Maybe they were loving and attentive when they were around, but also often absent for long periods of time. There were probably things about them that you thought were wonderful, and others that you found challenging, and it's OK to remember them that way.

Accepting that someone wasn't perfect and that your relationship with them wasn't perfect either isn't dishonoring their memory in death; in fact, it is honoring more fully who they were when they were alive.

You can hold conflicting feelings.

One of the many surreal aspects of grief is having seemingly contradictory thoughts or feelings: *I'm fine and not fine. I know they're dead and I can't believe they're gone.* These can feel impossible to reconcile—how can they be in opposition to each other and both be true? It can feel like we have to choose. But as confusing and difficult as it is, we are capable of holding multiple complicated truths at the same time.

I feel relieved.

I feel sad.

I know that everyone dies.

This feels impossible.

I want to move forward.

I don't want to leave them behind.

I knew this was coming.

I wasn't prepared for them to die.

Remembering them brings me joy.

Remembering them brings me pain.

I'm OK.

I'm not OK.

I miss them.

I'm so angry with them.

I know death is permanent.

I can't believe that they're not coming back.

I know it's not my fault.

I feel guilty for not preventing this.

I still love them.

I'm falling in love with someone else.

It's OK to Feel Many Things at the Same Time · 47

The case for joy.

In the depths of your grief, it can be hard—or impossible—to feel joy. Even when you reach for it, it can feel as if the place where joy used to reside now just houses more sorrow. It can seem like joy is forever lost to you.

But joy is irrepressible. Even in times of deepest despair, it eventually finds its way to the surface. At first, it appears in flashes—a peaceful moment in the sun, the slight upturn of a smile. Gradually, it shows up in more moments and stays for longer stretches of time.

Those first inklings of joy can bring a mix of emotions. They can come as a relief, a welcome sign that the acuteness of your pain is finally starting to abate and proof that you can still feel happiness. But if the pain of their death feels like your last remaining connection to them, you might wonder: *If I lose the intensity of my pain, will I also lose that connection?*

The pain of their death is not the only bond you have left. Joy also connects you to them through the happiness they brought to your life when they were alive. Maybe they always made you smile or laugh, or instilled in you an appreciation for music or food or travel, or taught you how to slow down and enjoy everyday pleasures. By continuing to find delight in the things you shared, you bring them forward with you, not only in your sadness, but also in your joy.

Joy is not at odds with our grief, but rather an essential part of our healing. Joy gives us a bit of relief when it hurts too much to keep going; it provides fuel to keep living. Joy reminds us what we're living for.

Let joy in. Embrace it. Seek it out and create more for yourself in whatever ways you can.

NOT ALL GRIEF IS THE SAME, BUT ALL GRIEF IS VALID

Inevitably, there are times when our losses get pitted against one another, as if we're forced participants in the Grief Olympics, and whoever is deemed to have the biggest, saddest loss gets to grieve the longest and hardest. Society often makes assumptions about which losses are worse than others—losing a parent is worse than losing a grandparent; losing a spouse is worse than losing a significant other; losing a sibling is worse than losing a friend.

But often a relationship is deeper, and the impact of its loss greater, than any title or label can convey. It's impossible for terms like "friend" or "partner" to capture the entirety of what someone brought to your life and what you lost when they died: the everyday moments and milestones you shared, your sense of safety and identity, your hopes for the future, and your understanding of the world and your place in it. There are no external measures that we can use to gauge, sort, and rank our loves and our losses. The only determination we can make is that each love is singular and special, and therefore each loss is uniquely hard.

So, let's cancel the Grief Olympics, give everyone a medal just for showing up, and stand together to honor everyone's losses.

IS MY GRIEF VALID?

↓

Did someone you care about die? → **NO** → It sounds like you're no[t] in the Grief Club yet. We're here if and when you need us.

↓

YES ↗ We're so sorry. Welcome to the Grief Cl[ub]

↓

BUT WHAT IF. . . → other people don't think [I] should be as upset as I [am]?

↓ ↓ ↓

I knew it was coming for a long time?

they were really old?

Grief is deeply personal. Just because someone else wouldn't be as upset if they were in your position (or think they wouldn't be) doesn't mean that you don'[t] have the right to be.

↓ ↓

There is nothing that can prepare us for the death of a loved one. Anticipation doesn't make this any easier.

Just because someone has lived a good, long life doesn't mean we can't be sad that they're gone and wish we had more time with them.

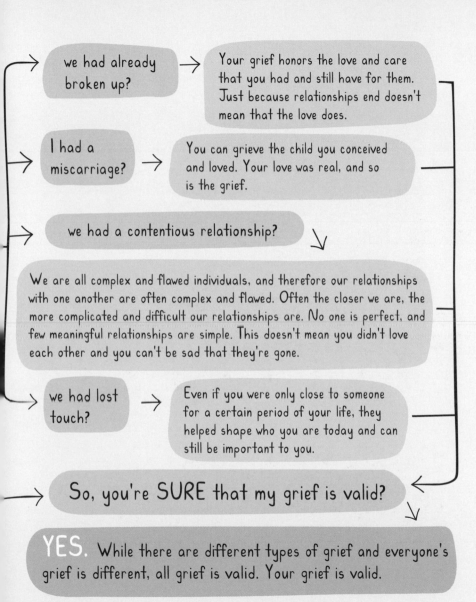

we had already broken up?

→ Your grief honors the love and care that you had and still have for them. Just because relationships end doesn't mean that the love does.

I had a miscarriage?

→ You can grieve the child you conceived and loved. Your love was real, and so is the grief.

we had a contentious relationship?

We are all complex and flawed individuals, and therefore our relationships with one another are often complex and flawed. Often the closer we are, the more complicated and difficult our relationships are. No one is perfect, and few meaningful relationships are simple. This doesn't mean you didn't love each other and you can't be sad that they're gone.

we had lost touch?

→ Even if you were only close to someone for a certain period of your life, they helped shape who you are today and can still be important to you.

So, you're SURE that my grief is valid?

YES. While there are different types of grief and everyone's grief is different, all grief is valid. Your grief is valid.

You get to decide the size of your loss.

Sometimes your loss is minimized or unrecognized by others if your relationship to the person who died is considered less significant, or their death is considered to be less distressing, than others. For example, if you are grieving a friend, a new or ex-partner, a pregnancy loss, an older relative, or a parent or sibling you didn't know.

An absence of condolences, sympathy cards, bereavement leave, and other acknowledgments of your loss can make you feel unsupported in your grief. You may feel like you can't grieve fully or openly without being judged by others. It might also make you question if you are grieving excessively, or if you have the right to grieve at all.

But it doesn't matter how your relationship was labeled or understood by those around you, or if it was recognized by society or not. It doesn't matter if it was short-lived, unconventional, secret, complicated, or went through different iterations. The only thing that matters is if it was important to you. You are the only one who knows exactly who you were to each other and what you lost when they died. If you feel a loss, that means that there was one. You, and only you, get to decide how big that loss is to you.

Regardless of who you lost, it's OK to miss them and to grieve the disappearance of a world that had them in it.

Hi you,

At your wake, someone asked me who I was, and I didn't know what to say. I never felt like our relationship needed a label; we knew who we were to each other, and that was enough. But then you died, and I don't know how to explain to people why someone they didn't even know existed in your life is so destroyed by your death. What we created together now seems to exist only in my head, and I'm questioning what it is exactly that we were, and what I lost.

I find myself desperately recounting memories as if I'm collecting evidence to make a case for us. I keep running through a list of all the little things I know about you, like how you thought most things could be fixed with copious amounts of Velcro and duct tape, and how you liked your coffee black but always remembered to add some milk for me.

I remind myself of how you always hugged me extra long whenever I returned from a trip, how intently you listened when I talked, how sincerely you apologized when you messed up, and how often you texted to tell me about your day, or to share a funny photo or terrible joke, or just to let me know you were thinking of me. I don't know exactly what that all adds up to, but it feels like love to me, so that's what I'm going to call it.

I love you and miss you so much.

xo,
Me

What if we had a difficult relationship?

It can be especially complex to grieve someone who caused you great pain, for example, if they were dishonest, mean, manipulative, absent, or abusive. There are often even more emotions added to the usual jumble, and your grief is more likely to defy your own and others' expectations of how you "should" be grieving.

You are allowed to grieve someone you disliked—or hated, even—or were estranged from. Give yourself permission to feel sad about the loss of a person who impacted your life, even if it was often in painful ways. You can also be sad about the loss of any possibility that they'll change or that you'll develop a better relationship with them in the future.

It's also OK if you don't feel sad, or if sadness is not your primary emotion. Maybe you had already worked through and come to terms with their behavior or absence while they were alive, or maybe you don't feel that anguished over the loss of a negative presence in your life.

Their death can resurface feelings of anger or resentment. In the same way that the impact of someone's love and care lasts beyond their death, the frustration and/or hurt that they've caused don't automatically fade away when they die. These feelings can be even more intense because your unfinished fights and open issues remain that way—painfully unresolved.

You might feel relief if their death makes you emotionally or physically safer. While this can seem like an inappropriate response, you have the right to be relieved or glad about the end of a harmful relationship.

You don't need to justify your grief to anyone, or hide or act out certain emotions in order to match expectations. This is a complicated situation— give yourself permission to have complicated feelings.

GRIEF HURTS, LITERALLY

Every part of you is reacting to this significant life event and trying to readjust to a new way of existing in the world. In addition to a cascade of different emotions, you may also experience myriad physical ailments from the stress and strain of grief.

Be kind to your body. Feed it and rest it as best you can, bring it outside every once in a while and move it around, take it home and plop it in a long bath or on the couch. And when in doubt, take it to see the doctor.

YOUR BODY IN GRIEF

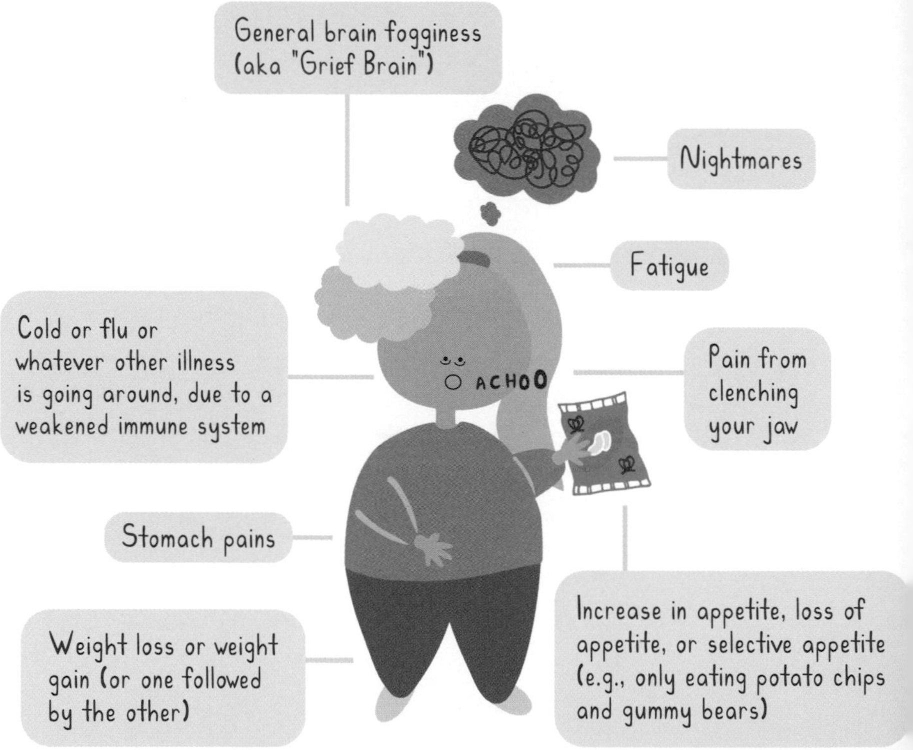

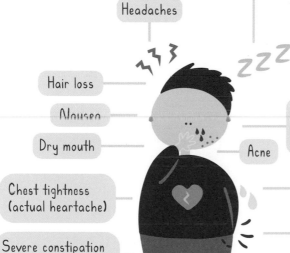

Grief Brain is a thing.

You may find that you suddenly have a hard time completing routine tasks or remembering simple facts that you wouldn't have had any trouble with before. It might feel like your brain is working overtime just to process everything grief-related and has dialed all other cognitive functioning down to a minimum.

These are signs that you have Grief Brain, yet another common but confusing and annoying side effect of grief. Show yourself some patience when you lose your keys for the third time this week and be liberal with your use of sticky notes.

Memory loss

Ack. We've worked together for four years, but I'm completely blanking on their name!

Hey!

Hey!

Absentmindedness

What is my toothbrush doing in the dishwasher??

Short attention span

As you can see here, BLAH BLAH BLAH . . .

Hard time following simple conversations

So, which one do you think is the better option?

I'm sorry, what?

Difficulty accomplishing simple tasks

I've spent three hours writing this email.

Hi all,

Can only do one thing at a time

Oh no.

Of course you're tired.

Grieving is tiring. Going about daily life is tiring. Going about daily life while grieving is fucking exhausting.

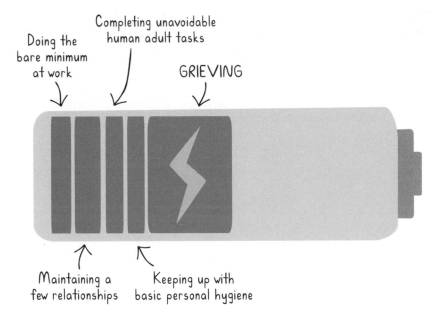

NOTE TO SELF: IT IS OK TO REST

Grief is not a sprint to the finish line; it is a lifelong one-person relay race. In order to keep going, you need to put down the baton once in a while and take a break. Rest until you feel like you are able to pick it back up again.

Sleep. Or just lie down if you can't sleep. Lose yourself in a bad TV show or a good book. Go somewhere with music loud enough to block out your thoughts. Walk around your neighborhood or in nature. Sit still and embrace the silence. Hang out with friends and only talk about trivial life updates and frivolous gossip. Welcome any momentary relief with open arms and without guilt.

You are allowed to pursue leisure. You are allowed to seek joy. It does not matter what you did or did not do today—you deserve to rest.

WEEKLY CALENDAR

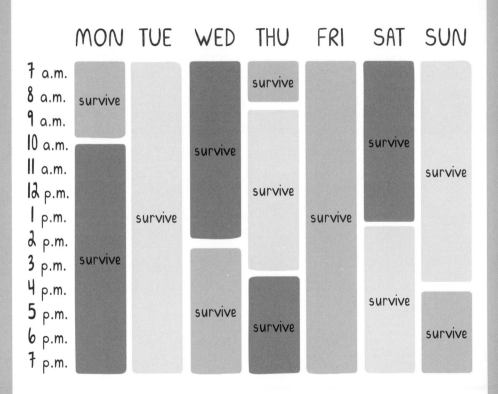

	MON	TUE	WED	THU	FRI	SAT	SUN
7 a.m.	survive			survive			
8 a.m.						survive	
9 a.m.							
10 a.m.			survive				survive
11 a.m.							
12 p.m.				survive			
1 p.m.		survive			survive		
2 p.m.							
3 p.m.	survive						
4 p.m.			survive			survive	
5 p.m.				survive			survive
6 p.m.							
7 p.m.							

WHAT RESILIENCE ACTUALLY LOOKS LIKE

We often think that being resilient means being able to recover quickly from any setback—to bounce back to how we were before without too much effort or disruption. When people say, "You'll get over this, you're so resilient," it can make you feel like you must live up to this expectation. It can imply that grief is something that can be overcome and set aside, if only you are strong enough to do so.

But our lives are irreparably different after someone we care about dies; there is no "normal" to return to.

True resilience is not a measure of your ability to be unyielding to events, but rather your ability to change with them. It takes fortitude to accept that your original plan is no longer the best—or even a possible—way forward, and that you need to find a new path and destination. It takes strength to feel the full extent of your grief, even if it knocks you off your feet. It takes courage to try something new, fail, and try again, and to ask for help when you need it.

Resilience isn't staying steadfast on a path that no longer exists. Resilience is doing the messy, hard, and slow work of creating a new life when the old one is no longer an option.

Everyday Acts of Resilience

Asking for help

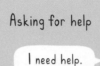

I need help.

I will stay for twenty minutes and then I can go home if I want.

Showing up for a friend's birthday party, even if it's only for a bit

Crying

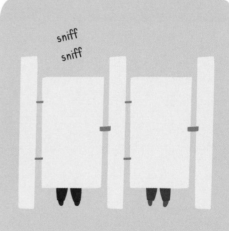

sniff
sniff

Still being open to love, even though you know how much it can hurt when they're gone

Going to work and spending most of your time hiding in the bathroom

PLAYING NEXT
EPISODE IN
3...2...1...
▶

Deciding that you are at your limit and
then watching TV for the rest of the day

Doing daily tasks
when doing anything
feels like a monumental
feat

Today I will
shower.

Taking small steps
forward, even if they're
imperceptible to most people

Saying no

I can't handle
that right now.

z z z

Taking a nap before trying again

I still can't bring myself to
go into that room.

Mmhmm . . .
Tell me more
about that.

Going to therapy

Even More Supremely Unhelpful Things
That People Say to Grieving People

What people say:

Don't cry.

You've been through worse.

I know someone who also lost a baby, and they're now happily pregnant again.

You'll be OK—you're so strong.

I thought you'd have put this behind you by now—it's been a year.

What the grieving person might hear:

Get over it.

This shouldn't be that big of a deal for you.

Dear friend,

Sorry I haven't responded to any of your calls, texts, emails, or letters. I did read them all, and I've been meaning to write back for a while now. The truth is, I've been unable to find the energy or will to do most things, including sending you a quick "Hi, I'm alive" text back, even though I know theoretically it wouldn't take that much time or energy to do so.

Someone brought over a rotisserie chicken, and I've just been eating it cold over the sink because I can't be bothered to heat it up or do dishes. So that's where I'm at right now.

I know you must be worried, and probably a bit frustrated by my silence. I would be too, if our roles were switched. But the longer I've waited to write back, the worse I feel, and so the harder it is to write back, and so the more I put it off. Please don't take it personally—I haven't really responded to anyone.

For what it's worth, it's been really comforting to see your missed calls, even if I never pick up or call you back. I'm not OK right now, but I know I will be. Please keep calling. Will pick up or write again when I'm able.

Love you,
Me

You do not need to experience post-traumatic growth.

Losing someone gives some of us a motivation and perspective we wouldn't have otherwise. Having experienced the intense pain of grief, some of us have a new sense of fearlessness when faced with other challenges. Struck by the unpredictability of life, others are motivated to spend the time they have left differently and pursue new places, people, and adventures.

It's also OK if you aren't channeling your grief into pursuing your dreams. Your grief does not need to be a source of inspiration, self-improvement, or success. You do not need to attend a meditation retreat, or summit a mountain, or write a book. Their death doesn't need to have a greater meaning. You will be transformed by your loss, but you don't have to feel improved by it. You are allowed to come out of the trauma feeling traumatized. You are allowed to simply survive and call it a win.

You are allowed to have struggles.
You are allowed to feel broken and too
shattered to pick up the pieces. You are
allowed to sit in the darkness for a while
and not immediately barrel toward the
light. You are allowed to not yet be able
to see the light.

None of this makes you a burden.

Life is really hard sometimes.
Everyone will struggle at one point or
another. We all take turns helping to
carry one another's burdens—
this is how we survive.

It's OK to share your sadness, even if you're sad all the time. Even if your sadness makes others sad. Even if you're difficult to be around. Let others help you. You do not have to hold it alone.

You do not have to be your best self to be worthy of care. You do not have to apologize for being a human who takes up space.

You are hurting and imperfect and deserving of love.

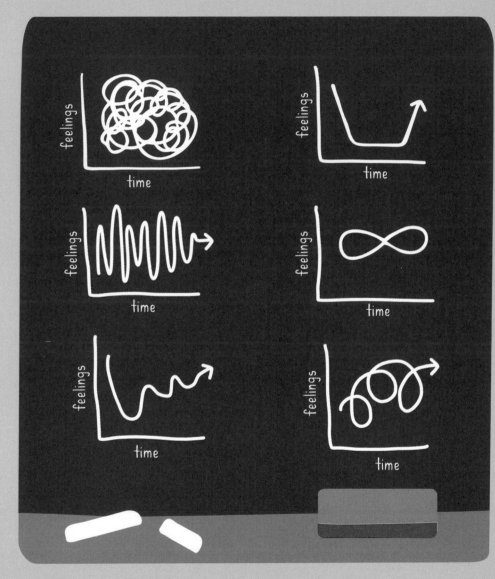

GRIEF ISN'T LINEAR, BUT IT DOES CHANGE

If only grief came with a road map that you could consult at any time to assess your position, track your progress, and prepare for whatever comes next.

Unfortunately, there is no straightforward path through grief—there are no stages that everyone goes through, or universal patterns or timelines for how it changes. Every loss presents us with a unique grief landscape, and we're forced to hack our way through uncharted territory every single time.

While there are no guarantees for how or when grief evolves, it does evolve. The journey through grief is bumpy with a lot of backtracking and detours, but eventually the jungle of emotions becomes less dense and treacherous to trek through, and there are more clearings to catch your breath and see what's ahead. You become better at navigating it, and while it's never easy, it does get easier over time.

EXPECTATIONS

Grief softens over time.

It can be hard to imagine or believe when you're in the initial depths of it, but the texture of grief softens over time. The weight of it lessens. The acute, all-consuming grief after someone dies eventually settles into a more enduring, less intense sense of loss.

This transition doesn't happen on a timeline, and sometimes it happens so gradually that you only notice it when you look back and realize that you are no longer in the same place you were before.

The triggers will keep coming, but there will be fewer of them, you'll be better at spotting them, and you'll be armed with the knowledge that you've survived them before. They may still reduce you to a heap on the floor, but they won't every time. At some point, you'll realize that there were moments or entire days when you weren't thinking about your loved one. And when you do think of them, the memory will make you smile without immediately making you cry. You will laugh, hopefully really hard. You will love, hopefully just as deeply.

While your loss will always be something that defines you, it will no longer feel like the only thing that does.

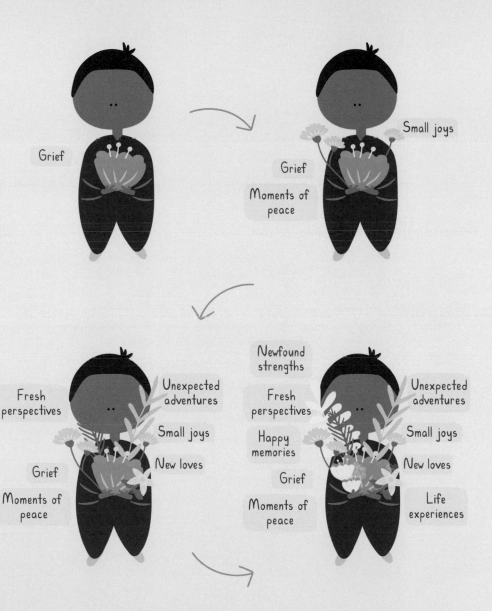

GRIEFLANDIA

OBJECT OF THE GAME

A ridiculously unfun game that takes you through a different grief journey every time. Starting at "Your Loved One Dies," roll the dice and move the corresponding number of spaces. There is no scoring system, no one wins or loses, and the game continues indefinitely.

ACUTE GRIEF ARCHIPELAGO

One of the most treacherous territories right after someone dies. Watch out for those Trigger Tornadoes! Contrary to common lore, you're not always in the clear after the first-year mark.

START HERE

YOUR LOVED ONE DIES

WHAT THE FUCK??!
Roll again.

No words.
Roll again.

Notify friends and family.
Skip a turn to recuperate, then roll again.

TRIGGER TORNAD
You have a dream about them.
Lose a turn.

Time to write the obituary—take a hike on **MEMORY MOUNTAIN.**
Roll again.

FRUIT BASKET FJORD

LONGING LAGOON, AKA THE "IF-ONLYS"
You're waylaid by intense longing for your loved one.
Skip a turn, then roll again.

TRIGGER TORNADO
You start to clear out their belongings.
Lose a turn.

CASSEROLE CITY

Eat the tuna casserole someone dropped off for three days straight.
Roll again.

Attend funeral everyth is a bl
Forget to roll a

First time going back to places you went together.
Move ahead one space.

First anniversary of their death.
Move ahead one space.

First holiday season without them.
Move ahead one space.

First birthday without them.
Move ahead one space.

IGGER TORNADO

You stumble upon some old emails.

Lose a turn.

FOREST OF FIRSTS

Unfortunately, you can't skip over this part—you have to go through.

LOGISTICS LANDING

Spend many hours on the phone with the bank, lawyer, insurance company, phone company, pharmacy, utility company . . . .

Skip a turn to recuperate, then roll again.

ON HOLD

Cry on some form of transportation.

Roll again.

KEEP GOING

TRIGGER TORNADO

Their favorite song comes on.

Lose a turn.

Someone sends you a kind sympathy card, and you feel less alone.

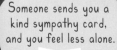

Move ahead three spaces.

WELL-WISHES WASTELAND

You'll often encounter this surprisingly soon in the midst of the Acute Grief Archipelago.

The cards, casseroles, and check-ins come to a stop as people return to their own lives.

Roll again.

INDEFINITE ISLAND OF GRIEF

Appears at some point after the Acute Grief Archipelago. True to its name, you can explore this island forever and never reach the end. You'll find fewer Trigger Tornadoes here, but you'll still encounter them from time to time. You may even find yourself back in the Acute Grief Archipelago for a few turns.

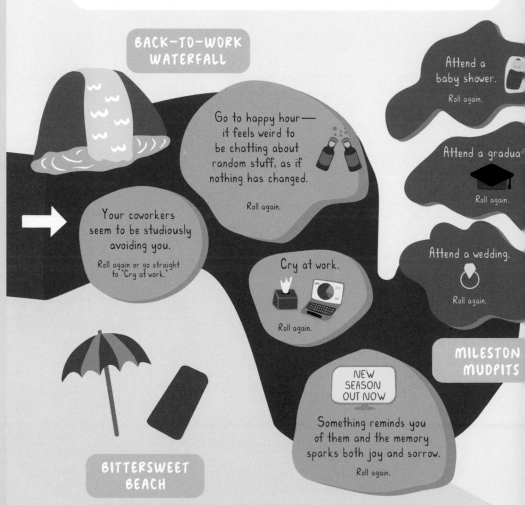

BACK-TO-WORK WATERFALL

Go to happy hour—it feels weird to be chatting about random stuff, as if nothing has changed.

Roll again.

Your coworkers seem to be studiously avoiding you.

Roll again or go straight to "Cry at work."

Cry at work.

Roll again.

Attend a baby shower.

Roll again.

Attend a gradua[tion]

Roll again.

Attend a wedding.

Roll again.

MILESTON[E] MUDPITS

NEW SEASON OUT NOW

Something reminds you of them and the memory sparks both joy and sorrow.

Roll again.

BITTERSWEET BEACH

TRIGGER TORNADO

Another birthday.

Roll again.

Another deathiversary.

Go back to **LONGING LAGOON.**

Make a new memory.

Roll again.

Have a really great day.

Roll again.

Have a really shitty day.

Roll again.

How are you?

When someone asks how you're doing, you say "Good!" and realize you actually mean it.

Roll again.

Randomly miss them really intensely.

Roll again.

WELCOME TO "THE NEW NORMAL"

DISCLOSURE DAM

JOY JUNCTION

Rest here for a bit, then roll again.

Tell someone new about your loss.

A memory of them pops into your head and it makes you smile.

Roll again.

So, where do your parents live now?

Roll again.

GRIEFLANDIA

The ripple effect of loss.

We generally recognize that death means the loss of a life, but we don't always anticipate all the implications of that loss.

Many of these implications become jarringly apparent soon after someone's death, for example, having to move to a new house, take on a caregiver role, find health insurance, or switch jobs or schools. These changes often reflect additional new responsibilities and losses in financial security that we may not have prepared for.

It can be hard to deal with decisions, logistics, and paperwork while you're grieving, especially since they often drive home all the different ways your life has been upended. It's OK to be frustrated. Take a deep breath, do what you can to address whatever is urgent, and remember that you don't have to do everything at once.

Some secondary losses ripple out from that initial loss over longer periods of time. The various roles that someone played in your life often become more apparent in that person's absence—you realize that you lost a go-to confidante, a coparent, an important source of physical intimacy, a financial safety net, or a primary connection to others. Moments like having to check "single" or "married" on a form, or when someone asks if you're a parent or how many siblings you have, can underscore the loss of parts of your identity. We lose pieces of ourselves and our lives that were tied to them.

In addition to grieving their death, allow yourself to acknowledge and grieve these resulting secondary losses. Give yourself time and permission to redefine new routines, roles, relationships, and ways of being for yourself. Give yourself credit for moving forward, one step at a time.

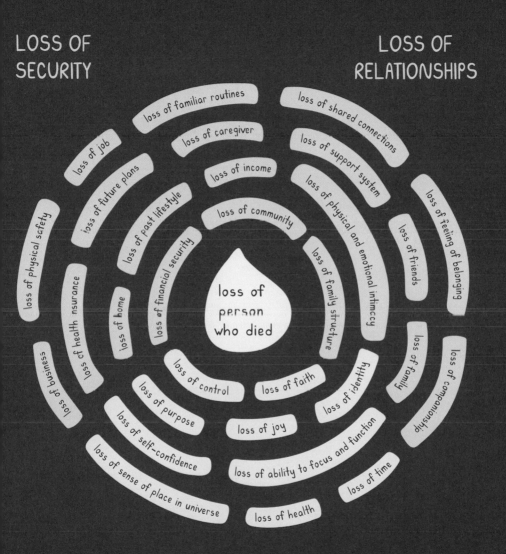

LOSS OF
SECURITY

LOSS OF
RELATIONSHIPS

loss of familiar routines

loss of shared connections

loss of caregiver

loss of support system

loss of job

loss of future plans

loss of income

loss of feeling of belonging

loss of physical safety

loss of past lifestyle

loss of community

loss of physical and emotional intimacy

loss of friends

loss of health insurance

loss of financial security

loss of family structure

loss of family

loss of home

loss of person who died

loss of business

loss of control

loss of faith

loss of identity

loss of companionship

loss of purpose

loss of joy

loss of self-confidence

loss of ability to focus and function

loss of time

loss of sense of place in universe

loss of health

LOSS OF SELF

Grief reshuffles your relationships.

Sometimes your friends and family will show up for you in full force, day after day, month after month, even after everyone else has returned to their own lives. Sometimes they'll know exactly how to help, and other times they won't know what to do or say, but their acknowledgment of what you're going through and their steady companionship can make the experience much less overwhelming and lonely.

THE STEADFAST ONE

THE FUMBLING-BUT-GOOD-HEARTED ONE

Sometimes people won't be present in the ways you expect or want them to be. Their absence can be due to a variety of reasons: they don't know what to do, they want to give you space, they want to avoid reminders (i.e., you) that they can also lose someone they care about, they don't want to deal with you when you're sad and "unfun," or they're just caught up in their own life events. They may not understand the magnitude of your loss or realize how much you're struggling. When someone pulls away from you in your grief, it can compound the feelings of loss and isolation. In some cases, an honest conversation about your respective needs and feelings is helpful; in others, you might decide they're not the right companion for this next stretch of your life.

THE INSENSITIVE ONE

THE ABSENT ONE

You may find comfort in your shared grief with others who are grieving the same person. Conversely, if you have conflicting ways of coping with your respective losses, that can cause tension and rifts in your relationship. If the person who died was the primary point of connection, you might cling together during the acute initial period of grief, but then grow apart as time passes.

THE ONE WITH SHARED GRIEF

THE ONE WITH COLLIDING GRIEF

You may also form new or stronger relationships. Acquaintances often reveal themselves to be fellow Grief Club members and can become critical sources of sanity and understanding. Others not in your inner circle—coworkers, friends-of-friends, or distant relatives—can surprise you with their willingness to engage with your grief and can end up becoming close friends.

THE UNEXPECTED NEW FRIEND

THE GRIEF CLUB MEMBER

Grief pressure tests relationships. It often strains them in some ways and strengthens them in others. Who shows up for you and who you find yourself instinctively turning to for solace and guidance may surprise you, and it is a reminder that in the midst of all the loss, connection and compassion can be found in both familiar and unexpected places.

When people offer to help, it's OK to ask for:

FOOD
- Drop off meals that are easy to freeze and reheat, or food that doesn't need to be cooked (fruit, baked goods, packaged snacks)
- Send gift certificates to local restaurants
- Pick up groceries

HOUSEWORK
- Do laundry
- Clean home
- Help sort through, dispose of, donate, or sell belongings

ERRANDS
- Pick up necessities—trash bags, paper plates, toiletries, prescriptions
- Sort through the mail and pay any bills
- Mow the lawn, rake leaves, and/or shovel snow

LOGISTICS + PAPERWORK
- Help with funeral arrangements, e.g., coordinate travel, choose flowers, create program or slideshow, write eulogy, choose funeral outfit
- Help with legal and financial paperwork, e.g., executing the will, closing accounts, paying any final bills and taxes

SOCIAL INTERACTIONS
- Run interference with funeral attendees and well-wishers
- Answer phone calls and text messages
- Write and send emails and thank-you cards
- Be a buddy (and escape plan) at social events

COMPANIONSHIP
- Just be around to listen, talk about it, not talk about it, cry, or laugh

More Things Grieving People Do That May Seem Strange but Are Actually Very Common

Preserve their rooms and belongings exactly as they left them

Laugh, really hard, sometimes really soon after they died

Remember that awful hat they used to wear?

HA HA!

Momentarily forget that they died

They're gonna love this story when I tell them later! Oh wait . . .

Keep and revisit voice mails, texts, and emails that they sent you

Hey, it's me, just wanted to see if you needed anything from the store. Anyways, see you soon!

VM
from 3 yrs ago

See signs from your deceased loved one

Be really emotional about other people's losses

LOCAL NEWS
Building collapses!
Small child loses kitten!
Man tells sob story at 8

Oh no.

Keep their number in your phone and call them to say hi

SPEED DIAL

Hey, it's me.
I know you're dead and all, but just wanted to call and check in . . .

Give away or sell their belongings

YARD SALE

Be haunted by the idea that you'll forget what they were like

I'm having a hard time remembering what their voice sounded like.

Take up (and get really into) random new hobbies

I know what will make me feel better! I'll learn how to knit and I'll make each of my friends their own special sweater emblazoned with their favorite animal.

There is never only one correct path. Any path you choose will be windy and bumpy at times, and longer than you think it will be. Any path you choose will also lead you to hidden wonders and spectacular views that you wouldn't have known otherwise. You will meet people and have experiences that will change your life in both wonderful and hard ways. All of this will be incredibly valuable.

You also don't have to stay on a path
just because you started out on it—
you can always get on a new path,
stay on it for a long or short while,
and then go on another different path.

The journey really is the whole point,
so pick a direction and go.

Whichever one you choose, you
are already on the right path.

THE RIGHT WAY

ALSO THE RIGHT WAY

CERTIFICATE OF ACHIEVEMENT

This certificate is hereby granted to

YOU

in recognition of your successful

COMPLETION OF GRIEF

Special honors for: concluding all visible signs of grieving within the allotted four-month time period

Signed: _____

GETTING ALONG WITH YOUR GRIEF MONSTERS

It would be nice if, at some point, you could declare that you are done with grieving, that you are, in fact, "over it." You have finally defeated your grief monsters and returned victorious, able to resume life as usual.

Unfortunately, grief isn't something that can be triumphed over. It doesn't go away, even if you want it to, or pretend that it has. You will never be "over" their death. In other words, your grief monsters are here to stay.

While you can't reach the end of grief, you can sustainably carry it with you. As you change, so will your grief monsters. While there will always be ones who are hairy and scary, you'll also find that others are content to hang out in the background or will show up hand in hand with joy. Your grief monsters can even become oddly comforting companions who will remind you not only of what you lost, but also of the love you had.

TYPES OF GRIEF MONSTERS: AN INCOMPLETE CATALOG

HAIRY + SCARY

HEAVY + SUFFOCATING

ALWAYS HANGING OUT IN THE BACKGROUND

Where we going now?

GRIEF

SMALLER + SOFTER, BUT STILL VERY PRESENT

GRIEF

Be right back, OK?

LEAVES YOU ALONE . . . BUT ONLY FOR A WHILE

Hey, wanna go to Sushi Station for dinner?

Sure, that sounds great.

Psst . . . that's the place you always used to go together.

POW

GRIEF

QUICK + SILENT GUT PUNCHER

Let's get some ice cream.

GRIEF

JOY

COEXISTING WITH JOY

Our hearts are clown cars.

Your heart has been stomped on, wrung out, and pummeled into an unrecognizable shape. There is no possibility of it returning to its original state, and the idea of it being able to love again should be laughable. It has been through too much.

And yet, despite it all, you have retained the capacity to love, and to love deeply.

Yes, your heart is now different, and so you will love differently than you did before. You might love more freely and fiercely, or more slowly and with more reservations. You might gravitate toward familiar types of love, or seek out radically different ones.

It can seem impossible that you will ever have enough room in your heart for all your existing loves and losses, and also for any new loves to grow. Won't your grief burden—and eventually destroy—any new relationships? Will a new love inevitably replace the one you lost?

Our hearts are clown cars—somehow they manage to accommodate more than we think is possible. Somehow all of our various loves evolve and rearrange themselves until the new ones comfortably coexist with the old. Instead of being in conflict with each other, they help us to appreciate what makes each one unique.

So when a new love comes knocking, open the doors of your already overflowing heart and welcome it in.

Grief and love last a lifetime.

We grieve because we have loved. Your love for them doesn't disappear because they died, but you have to learn to carry that love differently now— in your memories and conversations, and through rituals or however you choose to honor them. It shapes the life you make for yourself, and how you love others.

The persistence of grief is evidence of the love that still exists. How hard and painful and lucky it is that we have experienced love that lasts for a lifetime.

It's OK to take a break, even if you can keep going. You don't always have to test your limits—there is no shame in stopping long before you feel like you will break, in not choosing the hardest route if you don't have to.

There is strength in remaining soft in a world that hardens you. It's OK to fall down and not immediately get back up.

Sometimes you will crumple and still bear the creases even after you have uncrumpled yourself. You have not come out broken, but different. It's OK if it takes a long time to find your way forward—it so often does.

Love as well as you can.

A Closing Wish

There are so many things I wish for. Most of all, I wish Nap was still alive. I wish we had more time together. I wish he had years ahead of him to enjoy his passions and to discover new ones. I wish he had a chance to become the man I could see he was growing into. At the very least, I wish I had a chance to say goodbye and I love you.

Grief teaches us lessons. These are lessons that we never asked for or wanted, and the price is always too high, but they are lessons we learn nonetheless.

I wish I had loved Nap better when he was alive—that we had loved each other better. When I talked to my therapist about this, trying to simultaneously reconcile both our relationship and his death, she said, "He loved you as well as he could."

The more I think about this, the more I believe that is one of the lessons that matters most in all this—not that we love neatly or perfectly, but that we love as well as our deeply flawed, earnest, scared, selfish, insecure, broken-and-stitched-together hearts can. It is the most we can ask of one another, and it is the most valuable gift we can give. In my experience, of all the emotions encompassed in grief, love—imperfect, complicated love—is the most enduring.

There are so many wishes that are impossible to fulfill, and so many choices that are taken from us. But one choice we do have is to continue to lean into love, as terrifying as it can be to open ourselves up to it again when we know how devastating its loss can be.

I still don't really know how any of this goes or how it will turn out. In the face of more questions than answers, I hold on to what I've learned: Love is a common thread between the old world that we had and this new one that we have to forge for ourselves. It tethers us, but doesn't hold us back. It has a funny way of making everything better, even if in some way it's what caused us pain in the first place. Love doesn't fix our troubles, but it sustains us through them. Love gives us something worth rebuilding for.

So, with all of my grief monsters in tow, I've decided to keep on loving as well as my deeply flawed, earnest, scared, selfish, insecure, broken-and-stitched-together heart can.

I hope that you do too.

Acknowledgments

I am deeply grateful to my editor, Rachael Mt. Pleasant, who saw this book's potential when it was just a greeting card, and who championed and improved it at every turn. Thank you also to Janet Vicario, Terri Wowk, Beth Levy, Cristina Chua, Zoe Maffitt, Scott Trebing, Barbara Peragine, Claire Gross, Kate Oksen, Abigail Sokolsky, and the rest of the team at Workman Publishing who made this book a reality.

Thank you to Brianne Johnson for guiding me through much of this process, and for being in my corner. Thank you to Writers House and my agent, Stacy Testa, who jumped into the middle of this project with so much thoughtfulness and enthusiasm.

This book exists—I exist—only because I had people who stuck by me, and at times carried me, through the depths of my grief. They are still showing up for me in ways that I can never repay, but will always keep trying to.

To Nicole: Thank you for always supporting and loving me unconditionally. I'm so lucky to have you as my big sister, and will forever be grateful that there are two of us. I love you the most.

To Amy, Anna, and Jess: You had front-row seats to every up and down of this book, and held my hand and cheered me on through all of it. Thank you for reading innumerable drafts, responding to my sad texts, and making sure that I was always fed and somewhat showered. I wouldn't be able to do anything without you, and this book is no exception.

To Zenna: No one else is as relentless in their book edits or in their belief that I can do anything. This is a much more honest book because you encouraged me to critically examine my experiences, beliefs, and words, and to have conviction that the book I wanted to write was one worth writing.

Thank you for being my partner—being together brings me so much joy and makes me reimagine what is possible.

To Katie and Kathryn: Thank you for inducting me into the Grief Club with so much love and empathy, and for the free-flowing tears and laughter in the years since. I am eternally grateful for your friendship—both this book and I are immeasurably better for it.

To the rest of my chosen family—Arkady, Baird, Beeni, Jill, Kate, Mieka, and Rohan: Thank you for standing next to me and helping to raise me all these years, and for always making me feel less alone. All of my best parts are because of you.

To Bruce: Thank you for loving me like a sister, and for giving this book your blessing.

To Jennifer: Thank you for being a critical source of wisdom and compassion in my most acute period of grief. Much of this book draws from our sessions together, and you're the reason I tell everyone to go to therapy.

To my Kwohtations community: Without you, all of this would have remained a daydream. Many of you have shared your own experiences of love and loss with me—I hope you know that I see you and am honored to have been entrusted with your stories.

To other friends who waved flashlights in the dark—Alex A., Alex G., Alina, Alli, Amina, Carrie, Cynthia, Jeff, Jen, Lance, Libby, Roxani, Sanjay, Sheeren, my Dinner Party grief group: Thank you for being bright spots and safe spaces when everything was dark and scary; I will never forget your kindness. I hope you know how important you are to me.

To everyone who read an early draft: Your ideas, insights, and experiences helped to shape this book. I hope I did them justice.

Lastly, Nap, this book is for you. I think you'd be proud of me for writing it. I miss you lots.

About the Author

Janine Kwoh is the owner and designer of Kwohtations, a stationery company and design studio. Kwohtations is an ever-evolving collection of greeting cards and gifts that reflect and celebrate a diversity of identities and life experiences, always with humor and empathy. Janine's hope is that others will recognize some of themselves in what she creates and feel a bit more seen, more connected, and less alone.

While Janine doesn't have any formal training in writing or illustration, she believes you can learn how to do anything by reading the internet and asking for help. Exhibit A: this book. When she's not printing cards or writing about grief, you can often find her trying to keep her ducks in a row, but one of them is always wandering off in search of snacks.

Janine currently lives in Brooklyn, New York, but considers home to be wherever her friends are.

You can find her and her work online at kwohtations.com.